color these a**holes.

volume one

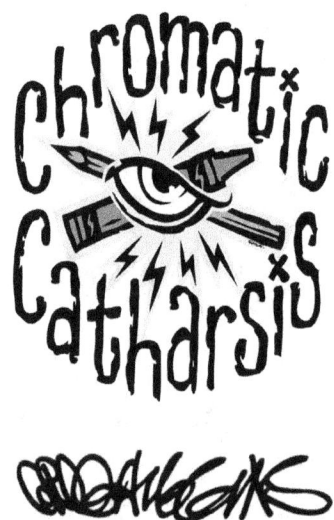

Copyright © 2018 by Greg Higgins

All rights reserved. No part of this book may be reproduced or transmitted in any form or by any means, electronic or mechanical, including photocopying, recording, or by any information storage and retrieval system without the written permission of the author, except where permitted by law.

Published by
Greg Higgins / Chromatic Catharsis
Portland, Oregon
greghigginsart.com

ISBN-13: 978-1985175679

"If you want to tell people the truth,
make them laugh,
otherwise they'll kill you."
~Oscar Wilde

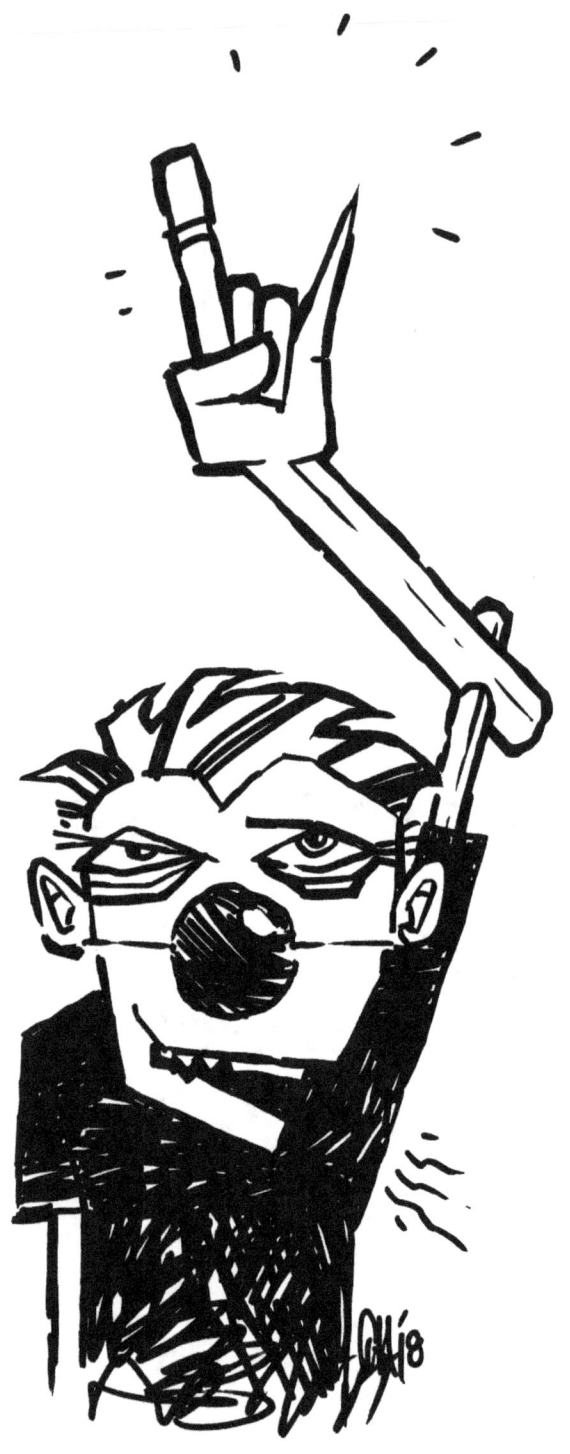

About the asshole who drew this book:

Greg Higgins was born and raised on BMX, skateboarding and Punk Rock in fabulous 1970's-80's Las Vegas and now calls Portland, Oregon home. Caricature bordering on portraiture is a common theme, as is improvisation, documentary, the play of humor in the face of adversity, dark humor, and absurdity. A self-taught practitioner of multiple media, he works prolifically in illustration, graphic design, pinstriping, hand-painted signage, murals and goods.

The inspiration for this coloring book stems basically from just watching the news, really - what more would I need? I am a firm believer in art as a vehicle by which to vent frustration as much as it is a conduit for passion, fear, neurosis, and whatever the hell else. When I got the news, I was just one of many that were shocked, stunned, confused, and pissed. With the exception of endless joke fodder for late night talk shows/comedy specials/etc, I found a lack of materials for people to blow off steam; I drew this book to help that along. So stay inside the lines, or go outside the lines. Color so aggressively that your crayons/pencils/markers bust in half, but by all means have a laugh and a good time with it. And use lots of orange.

- Greg Higgins

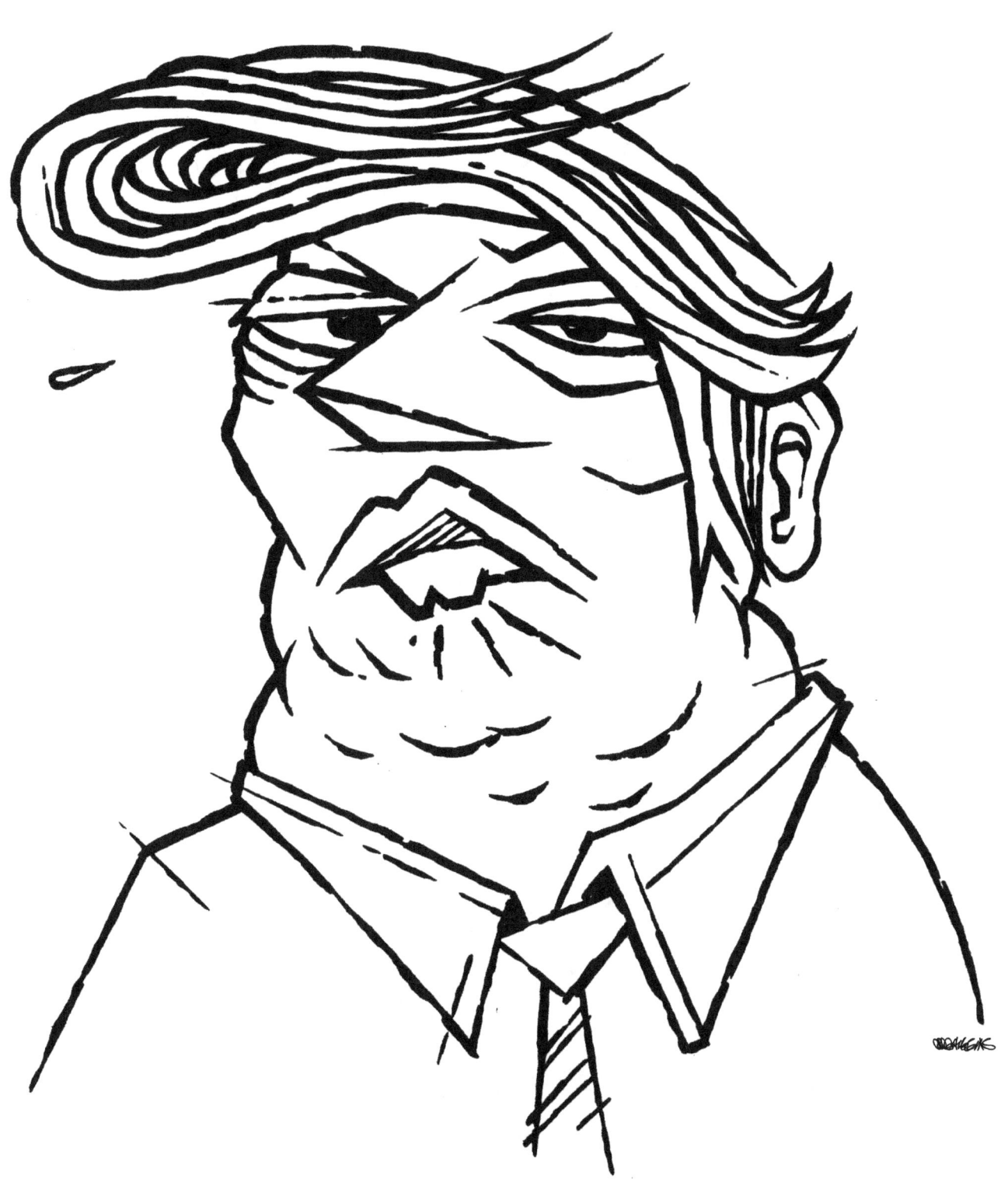

Color this asshole who threw paper towels into a crowd of hurricane victims in Puerto Rico.

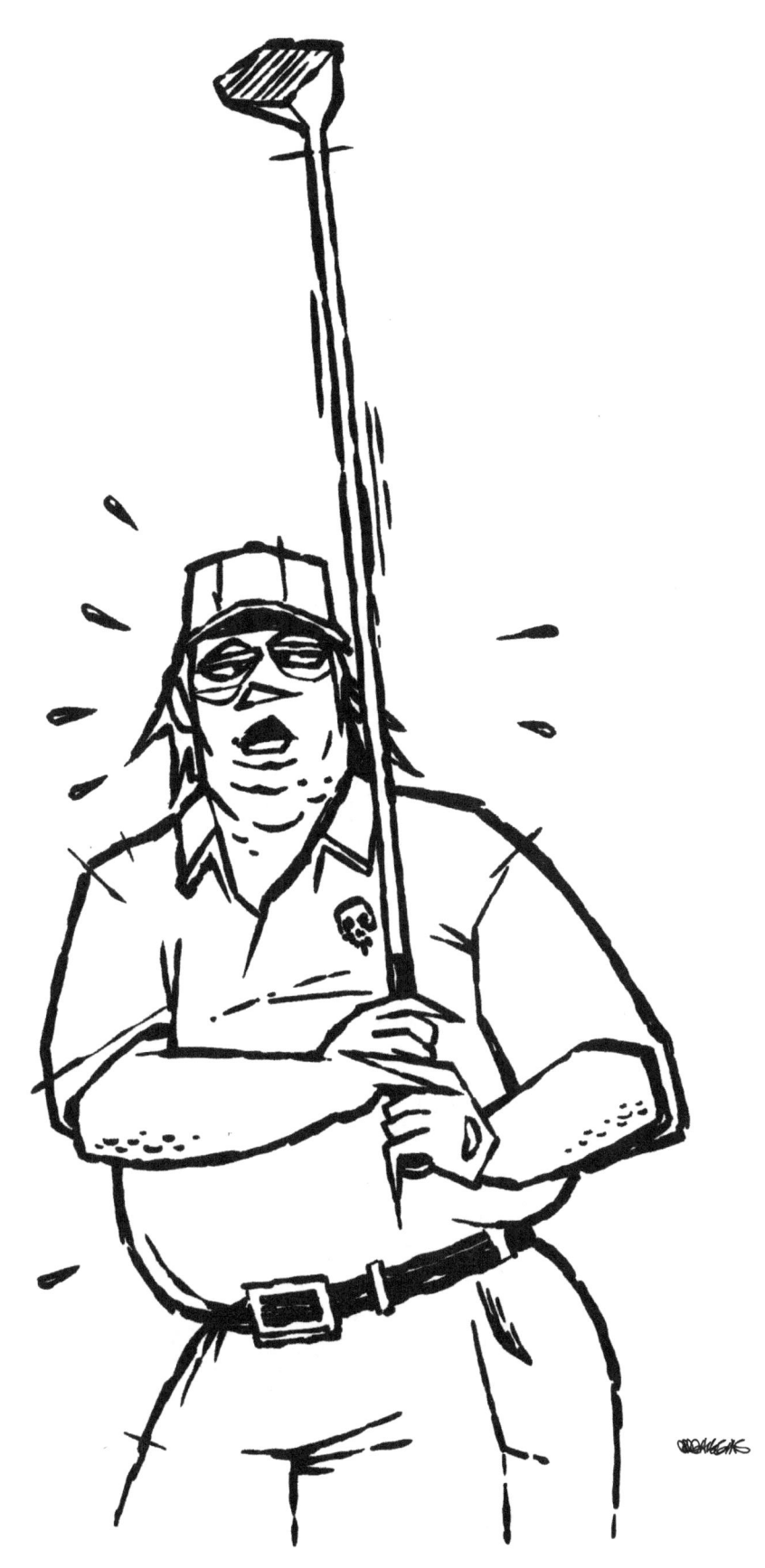

Color this asshole who spent MLK day golfing.

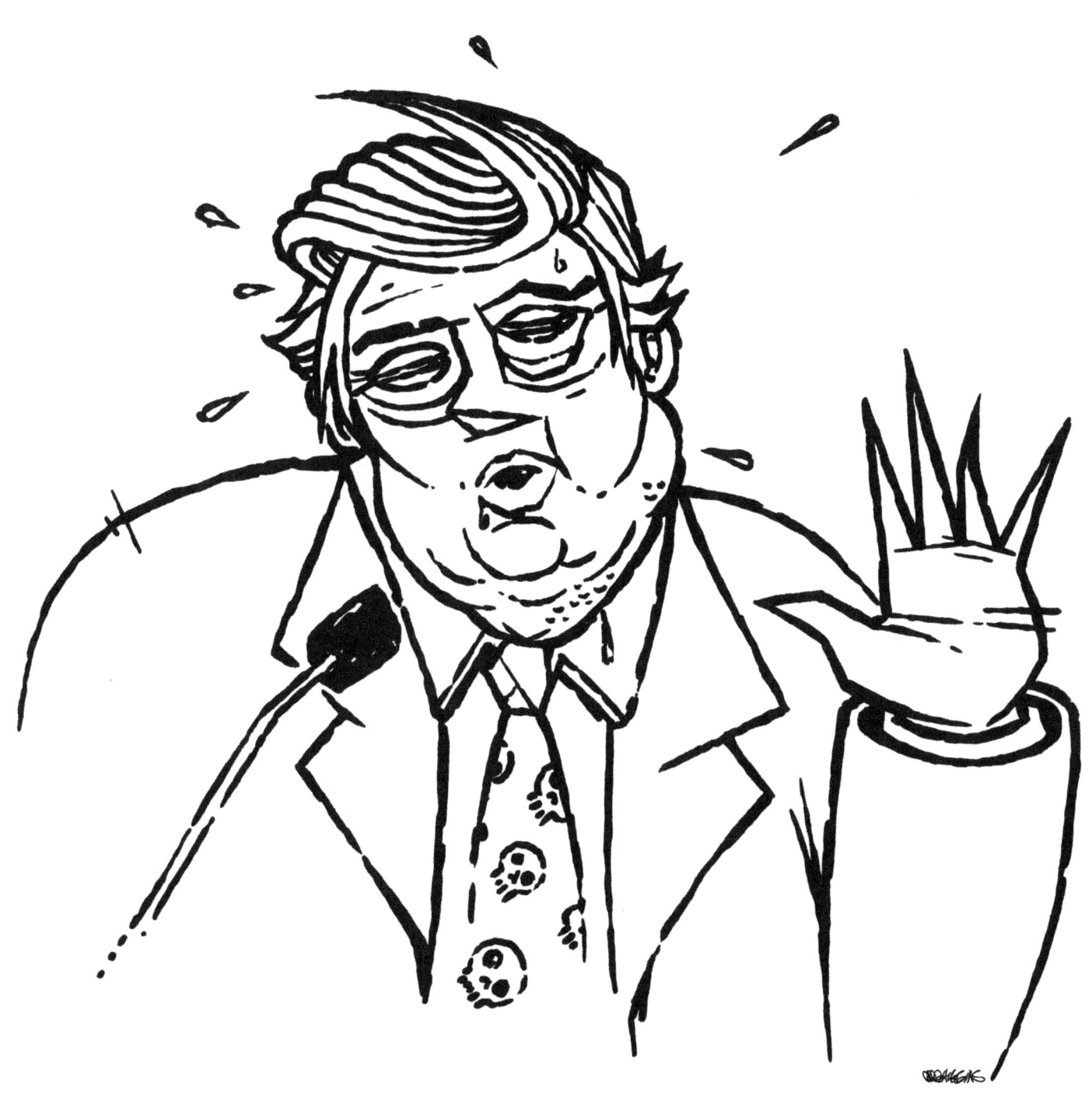

"Fake news is at an all time high. Where is their apology to me for all of the incorrect stories?"

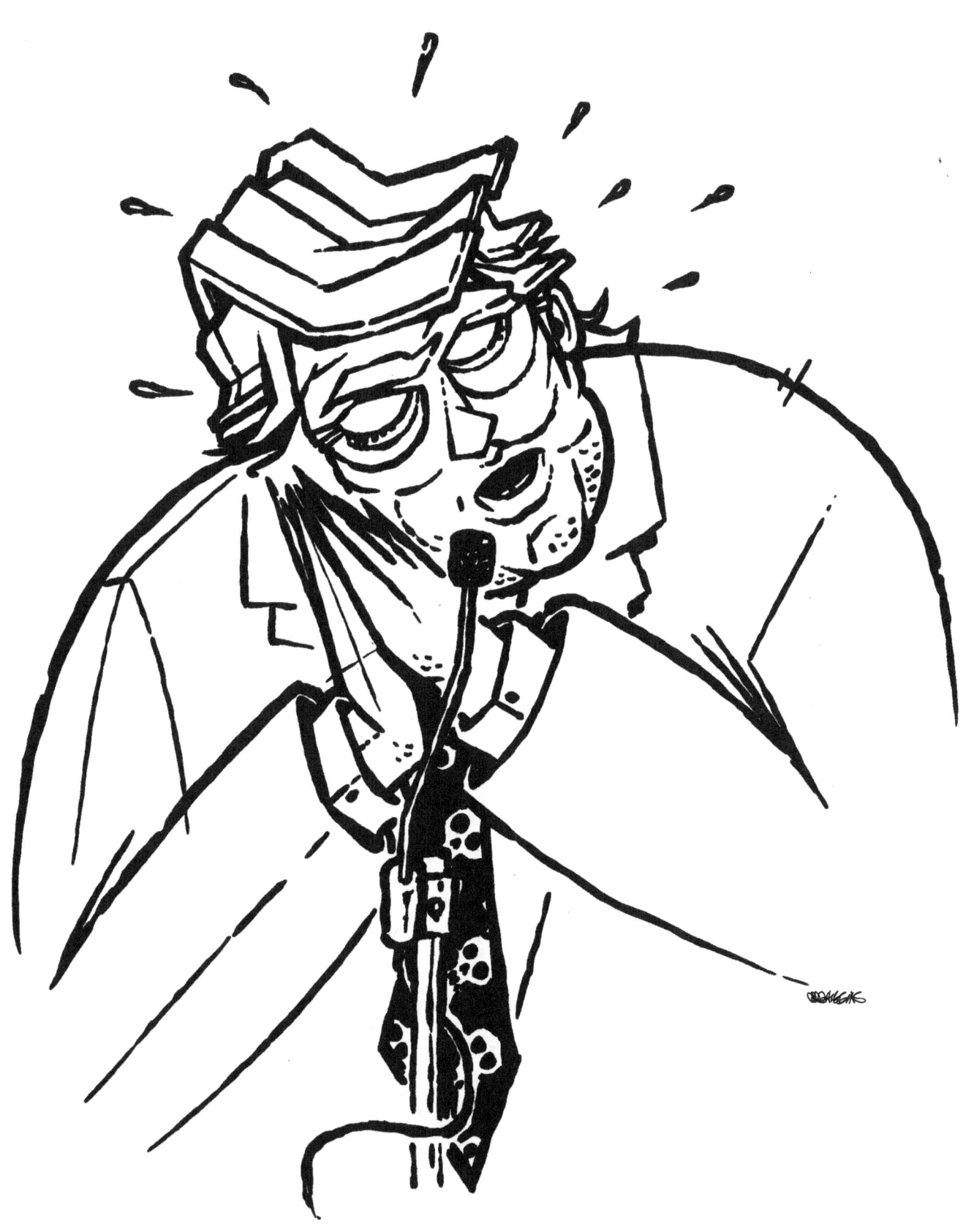

Color this asshole who is largely believed to suffer from the effects of sleep deprivation.

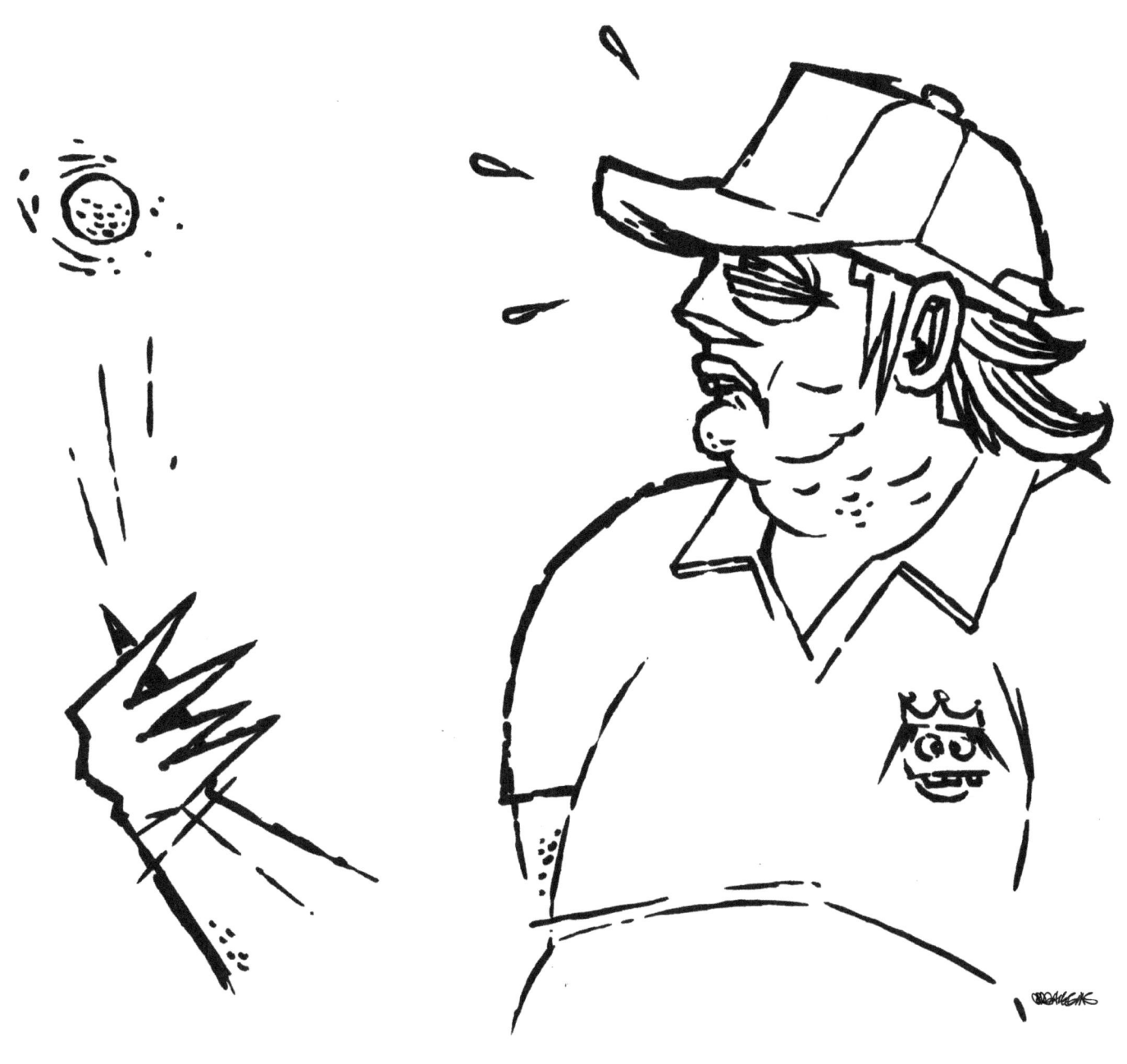

Color this asshole who said: "I will build a great wall-- and nobody builds better walls than me, believe me-- and I'll build them very inexpensively. I will build a great, great wall on our southern border, and I will make Mexico pay for that wall. Mark my words."

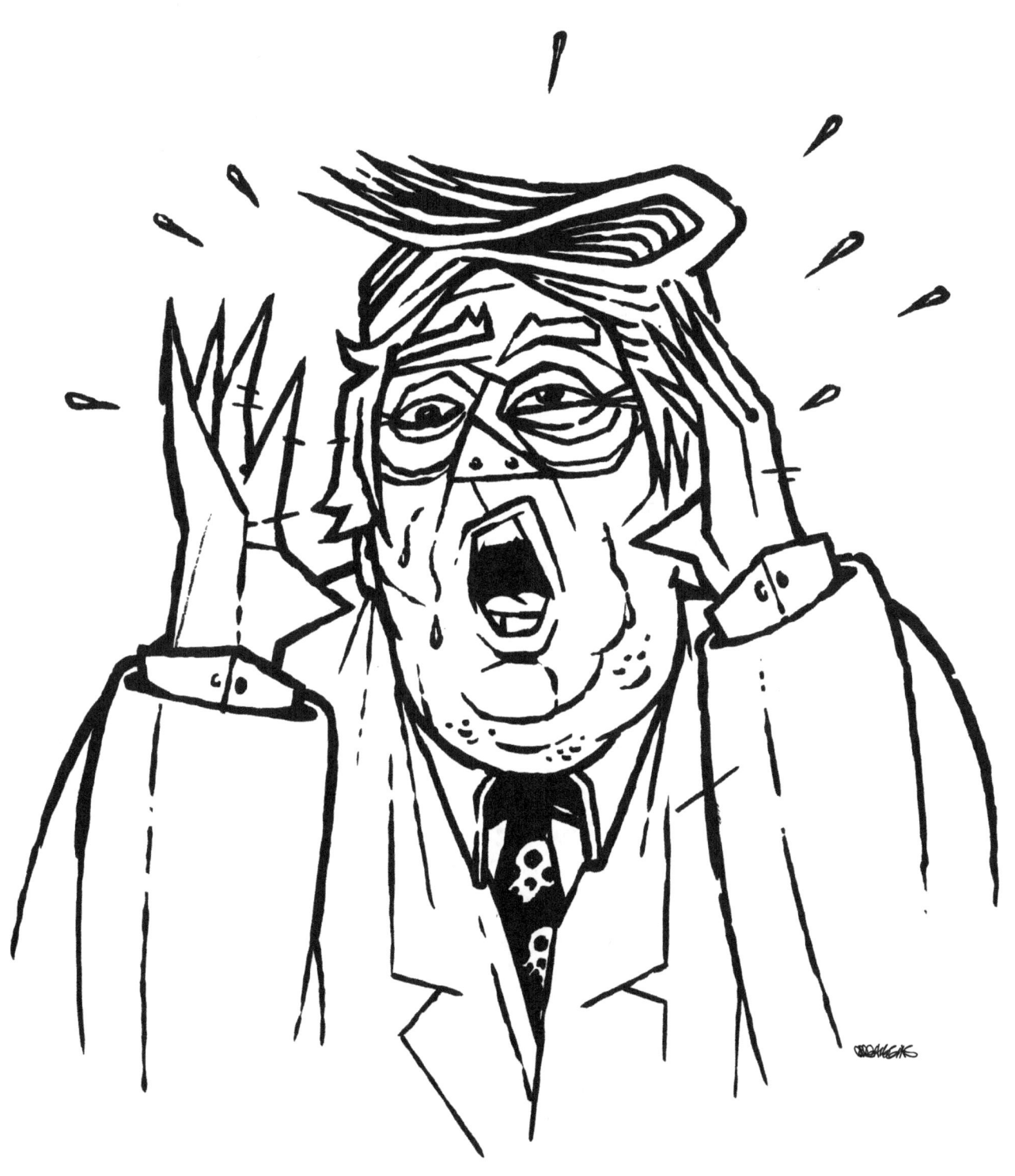

Color this asshole who claims to be a "very stable genius."

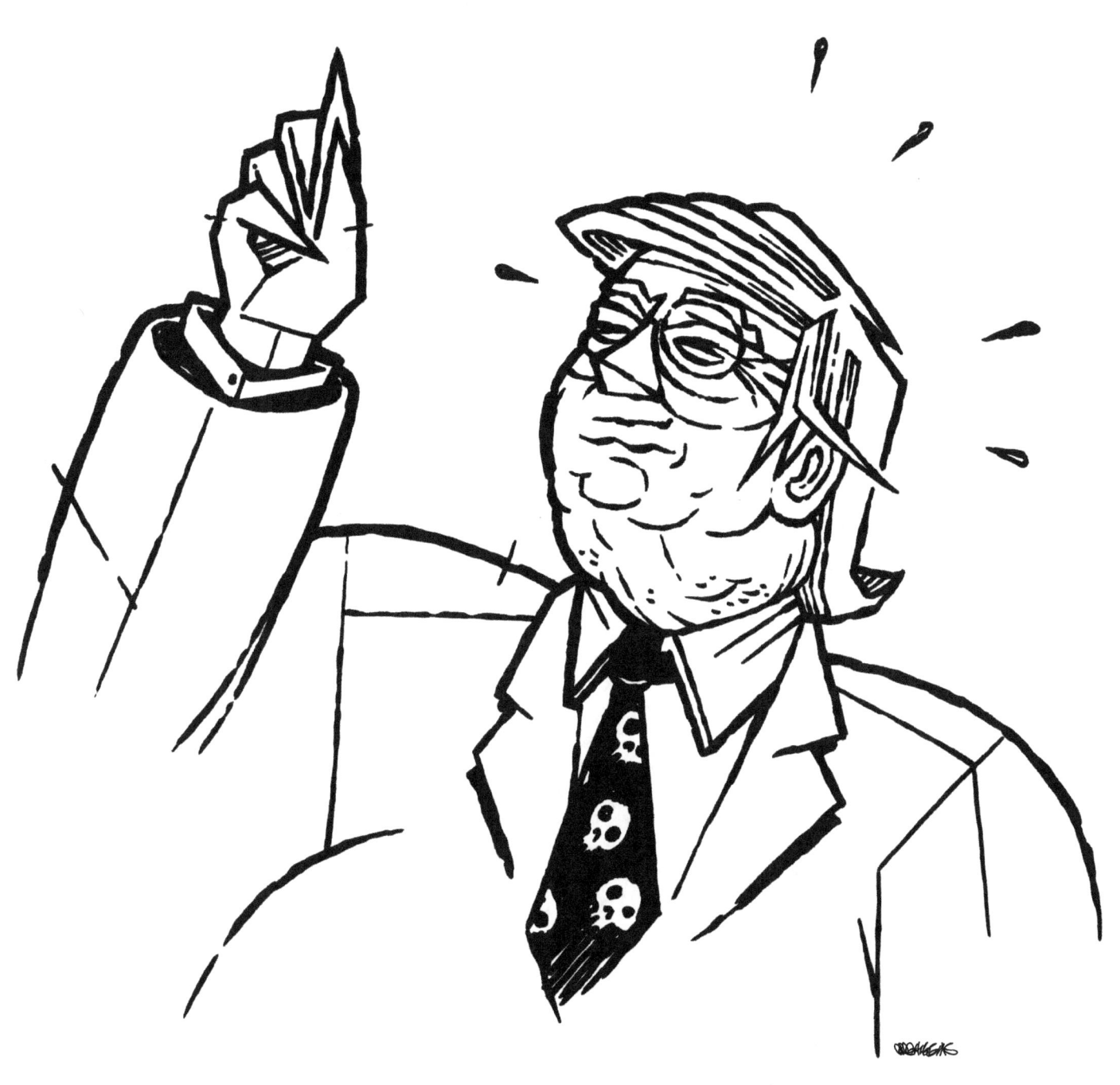

Color this asshole who looked at a solar eclipse.

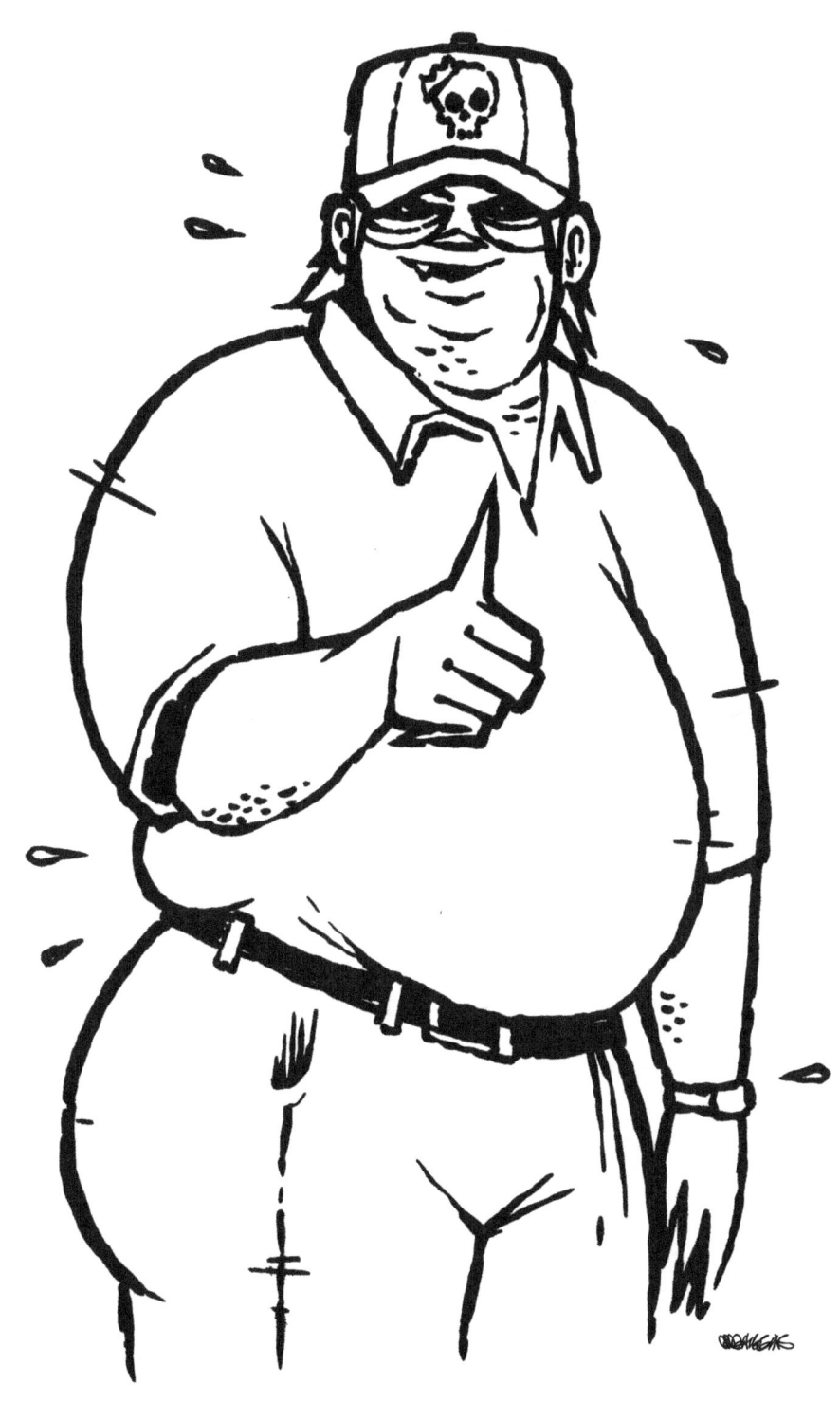

"My IQ is one of the highest--and you all know it! Please don't feel stupid or insecure; it's not your fault."

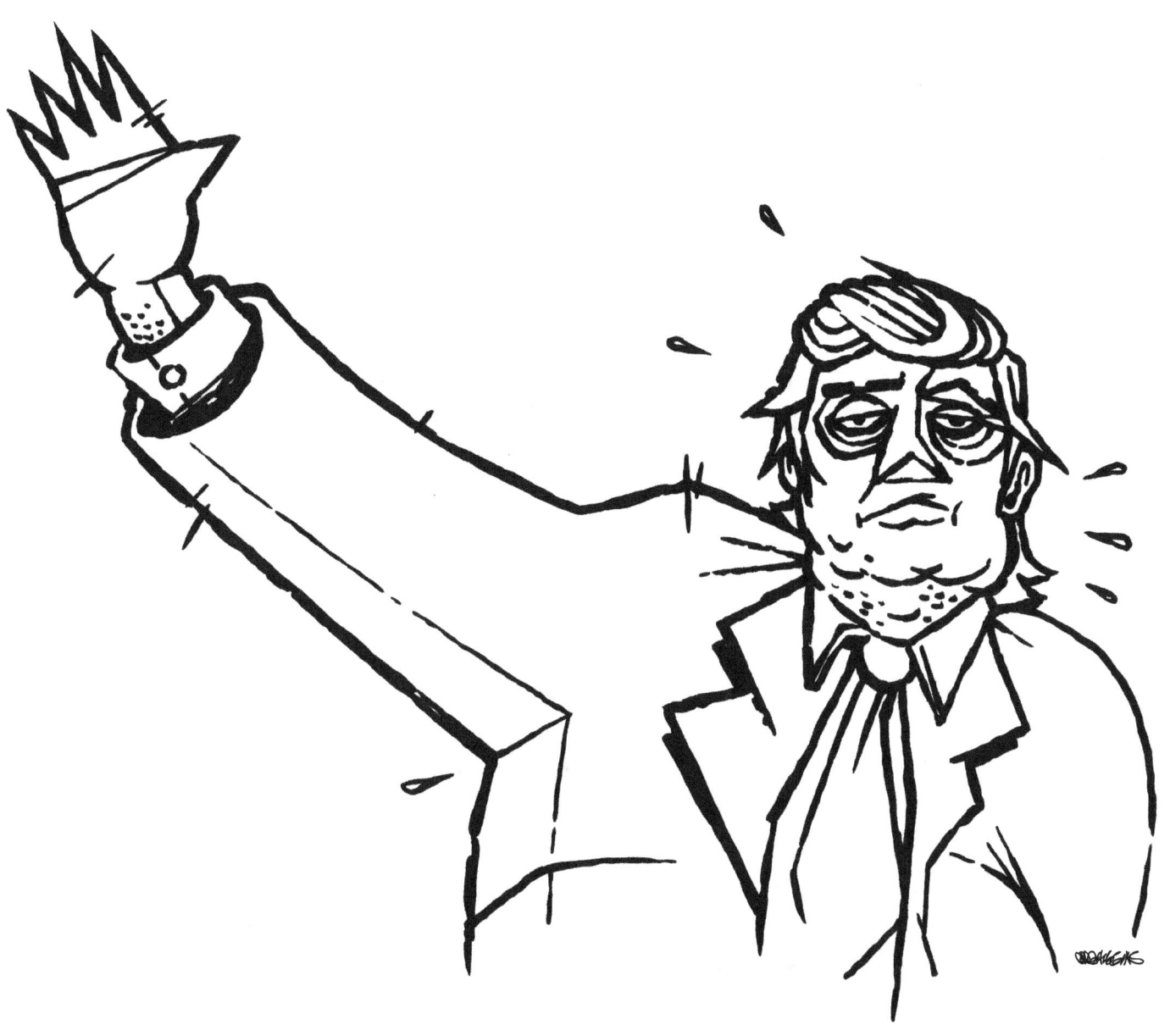

Color this asshole who, after an American serviceman gave him his Purple Heart at a rally to show his support, said "I always wanted to get the Purple Heart. This was much easier."

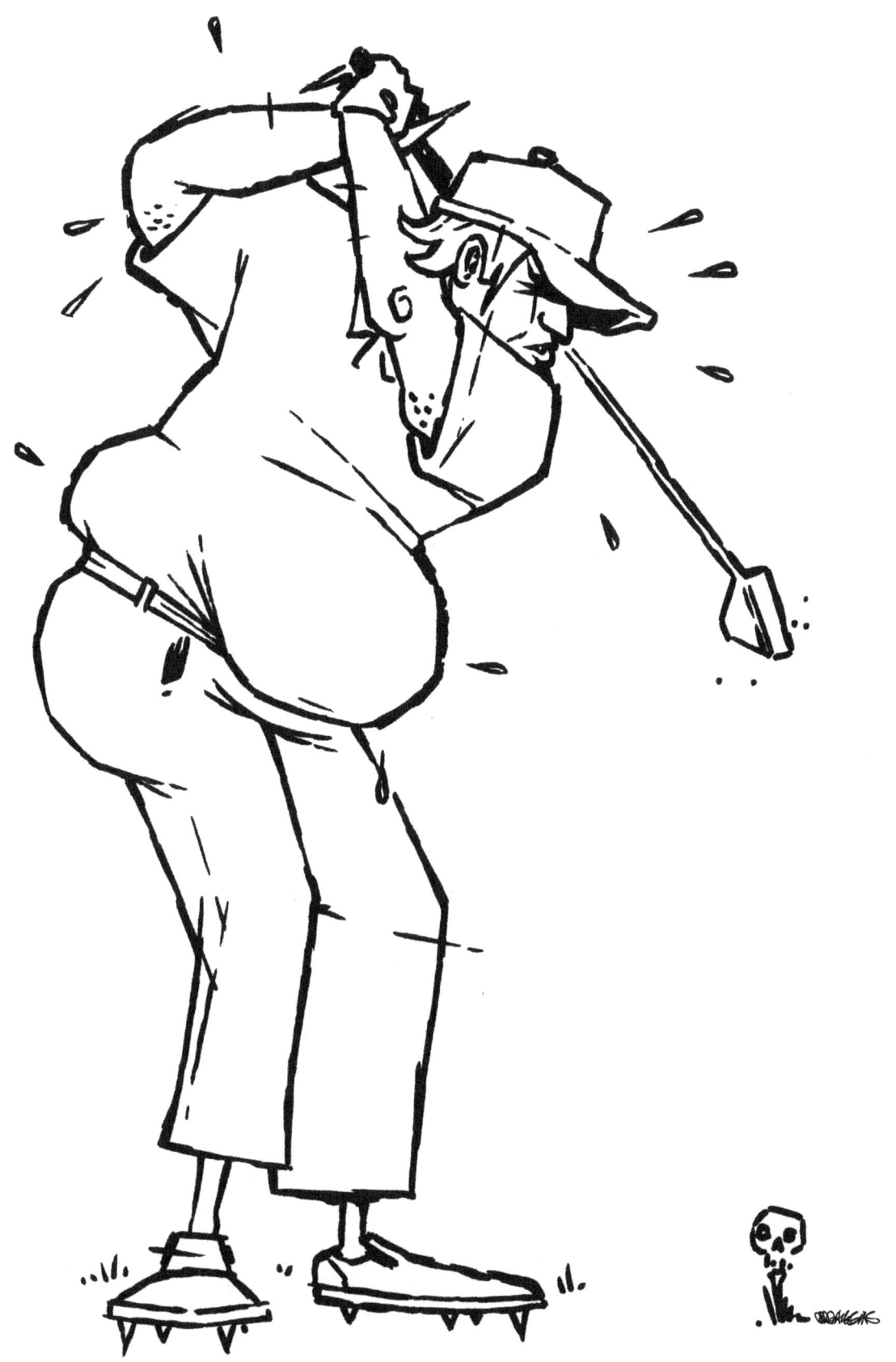

Color this asshole who supports the privatization of the prison industry.

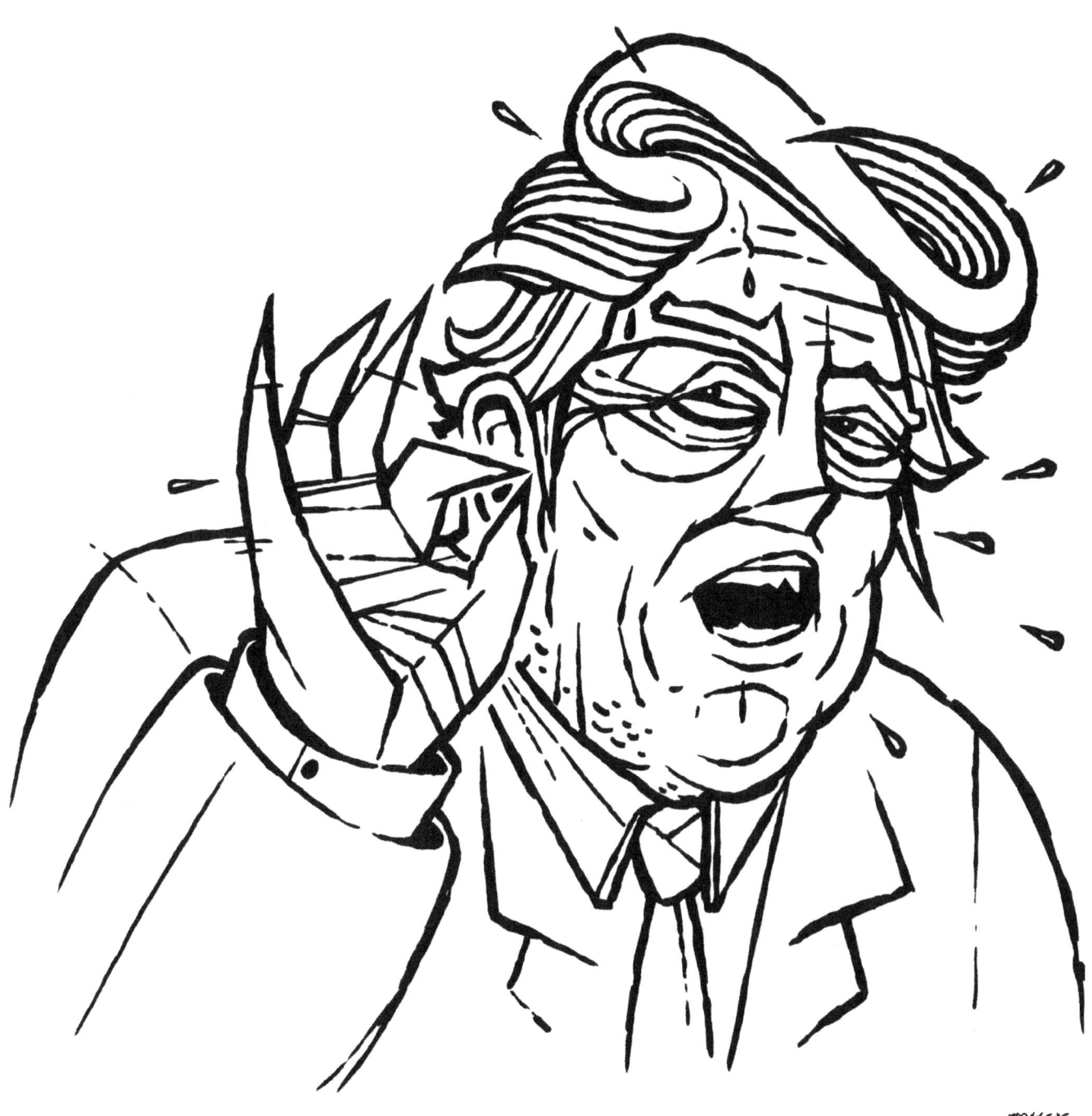

Color this asshole who proposed a budget plan that would eliminate the National Endowment for the Arts, the National Endowment for the Humanities, the Institute of Museum and Library Services, and the Corporation for Public Broadcasting.

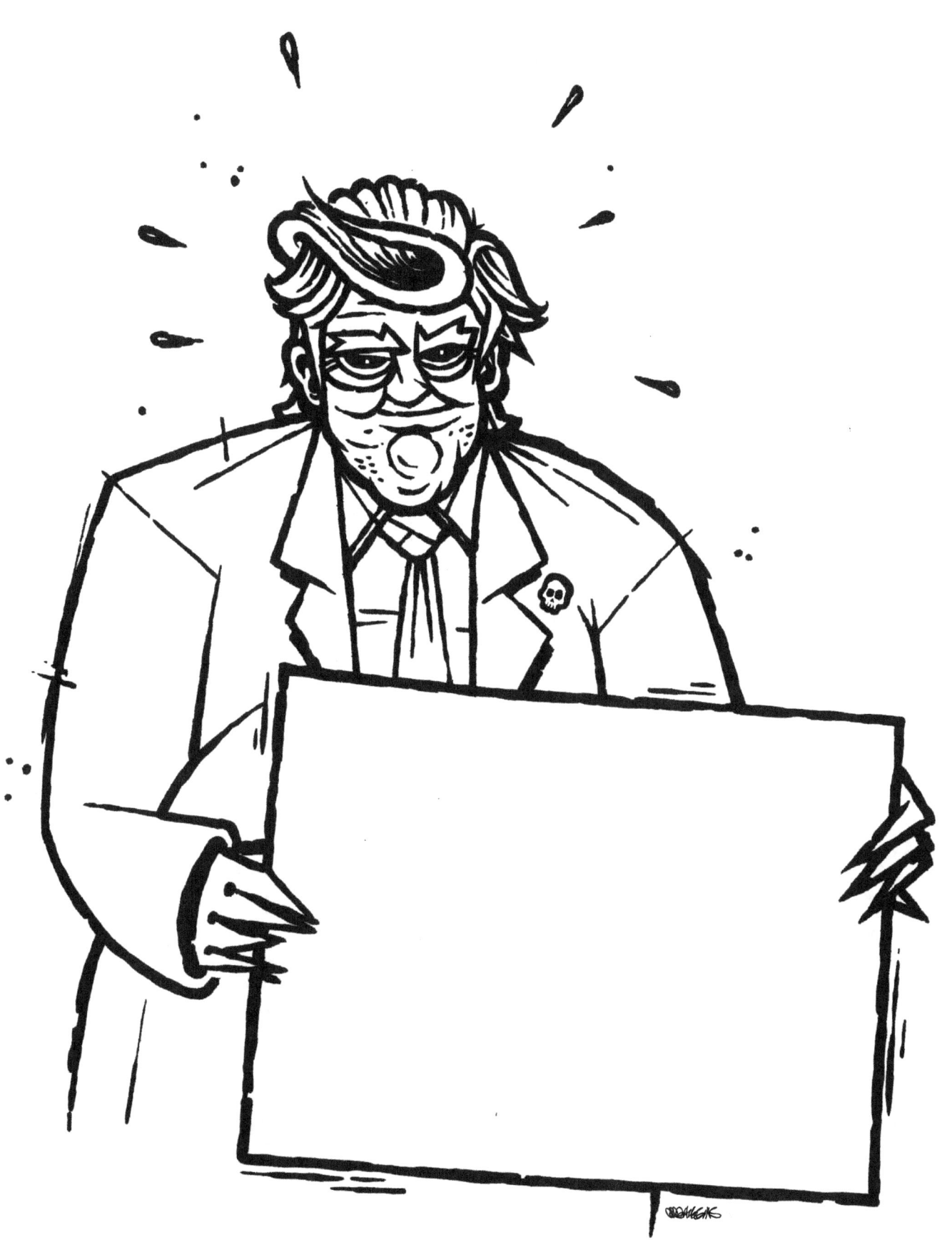

Color this asshole's sign however you see fit.

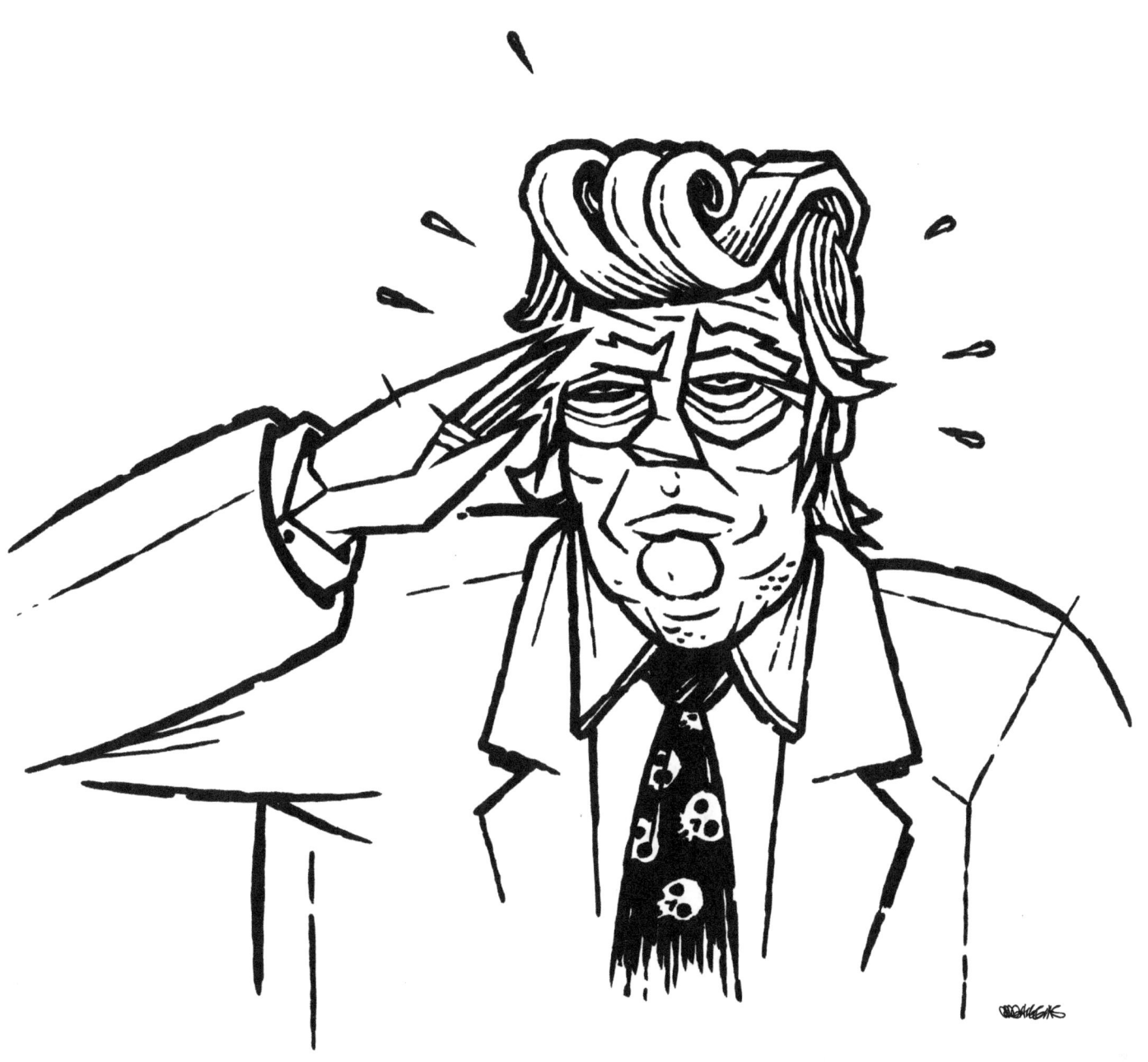

Color this asshole who maintains a long history of disrespecting, insulting, and patronizing American military service members and veterans.

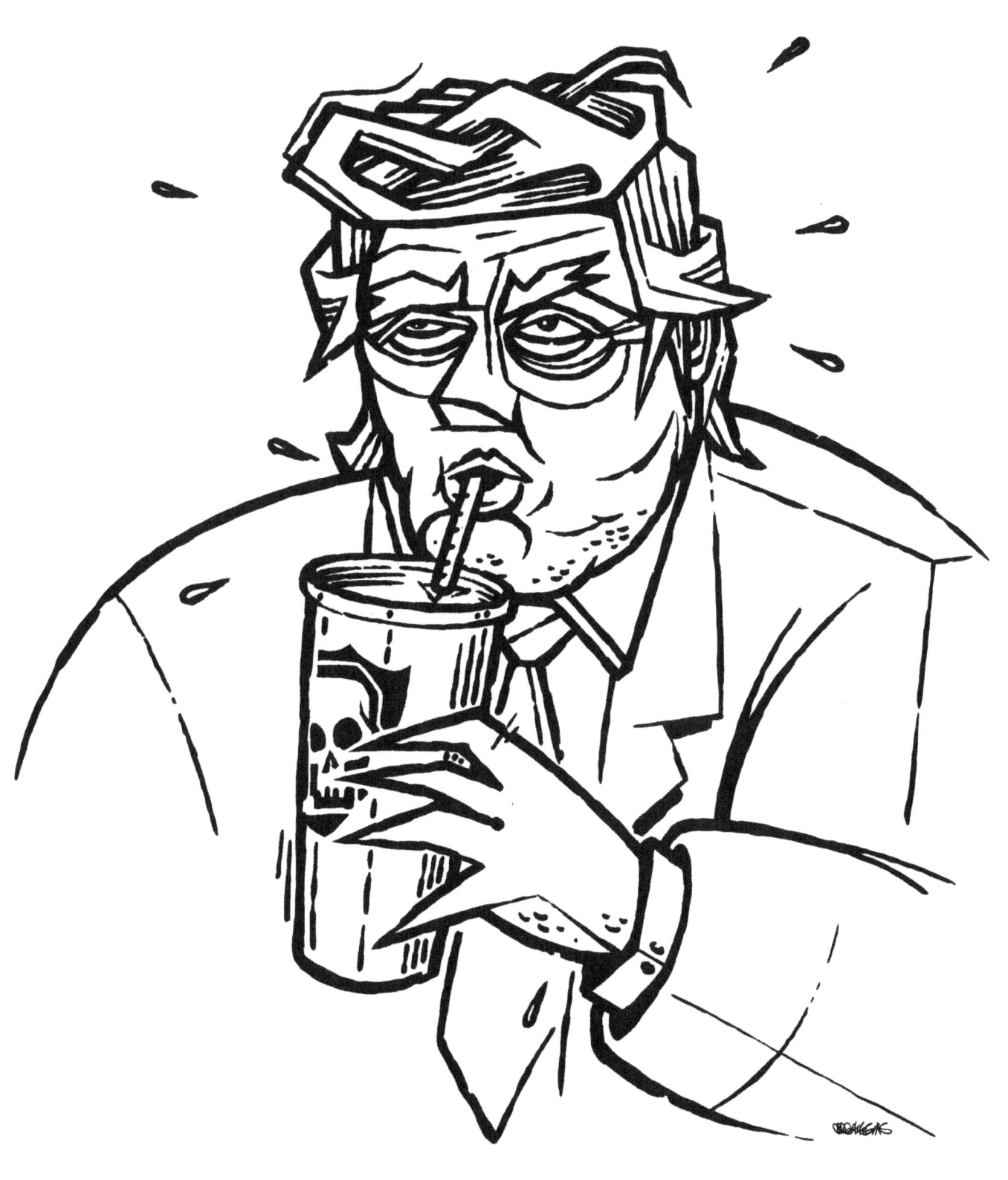

"Nobody knows the game better than I do."

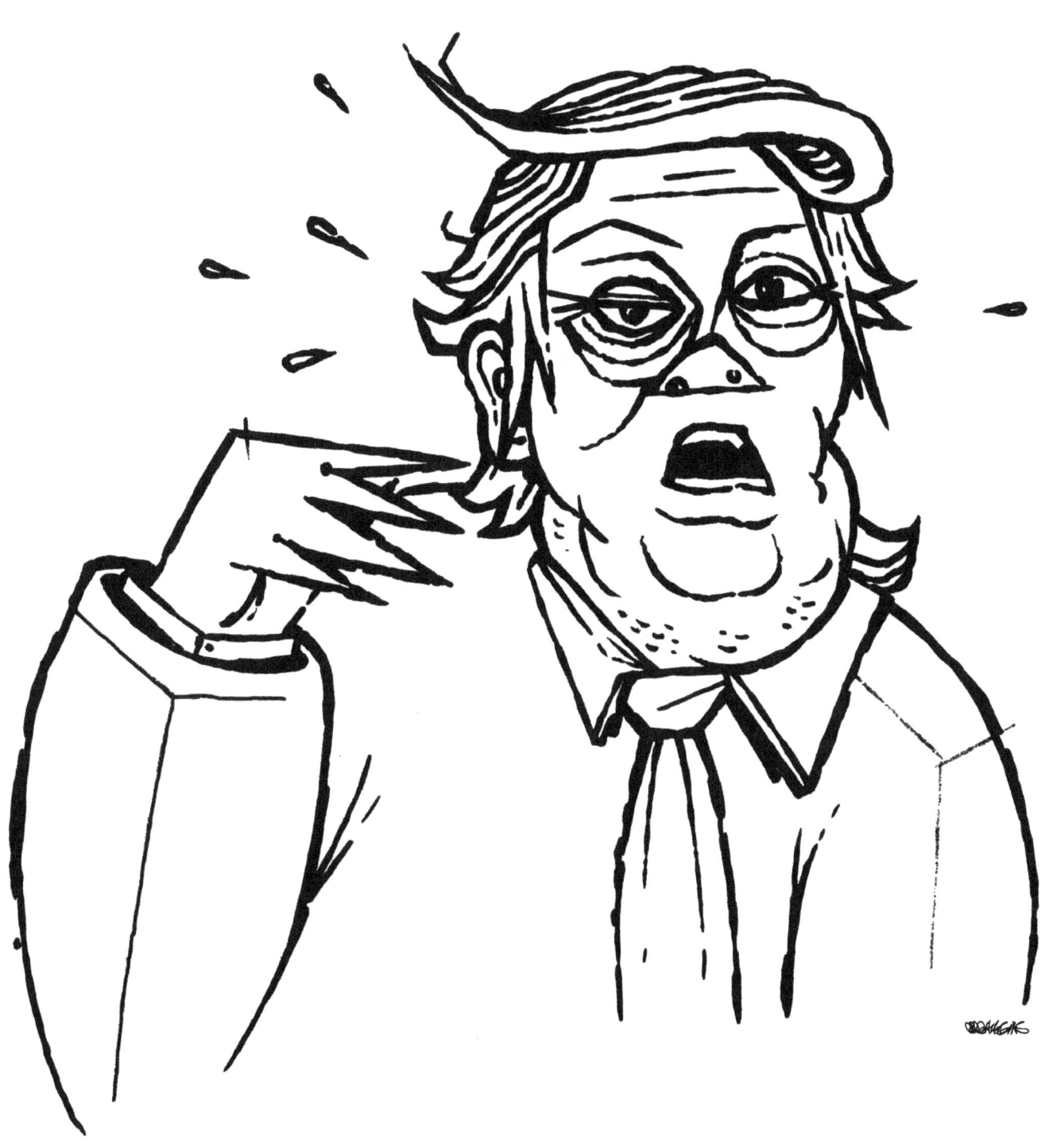

Color this asshole who blatantly mocked a disabled reporter.

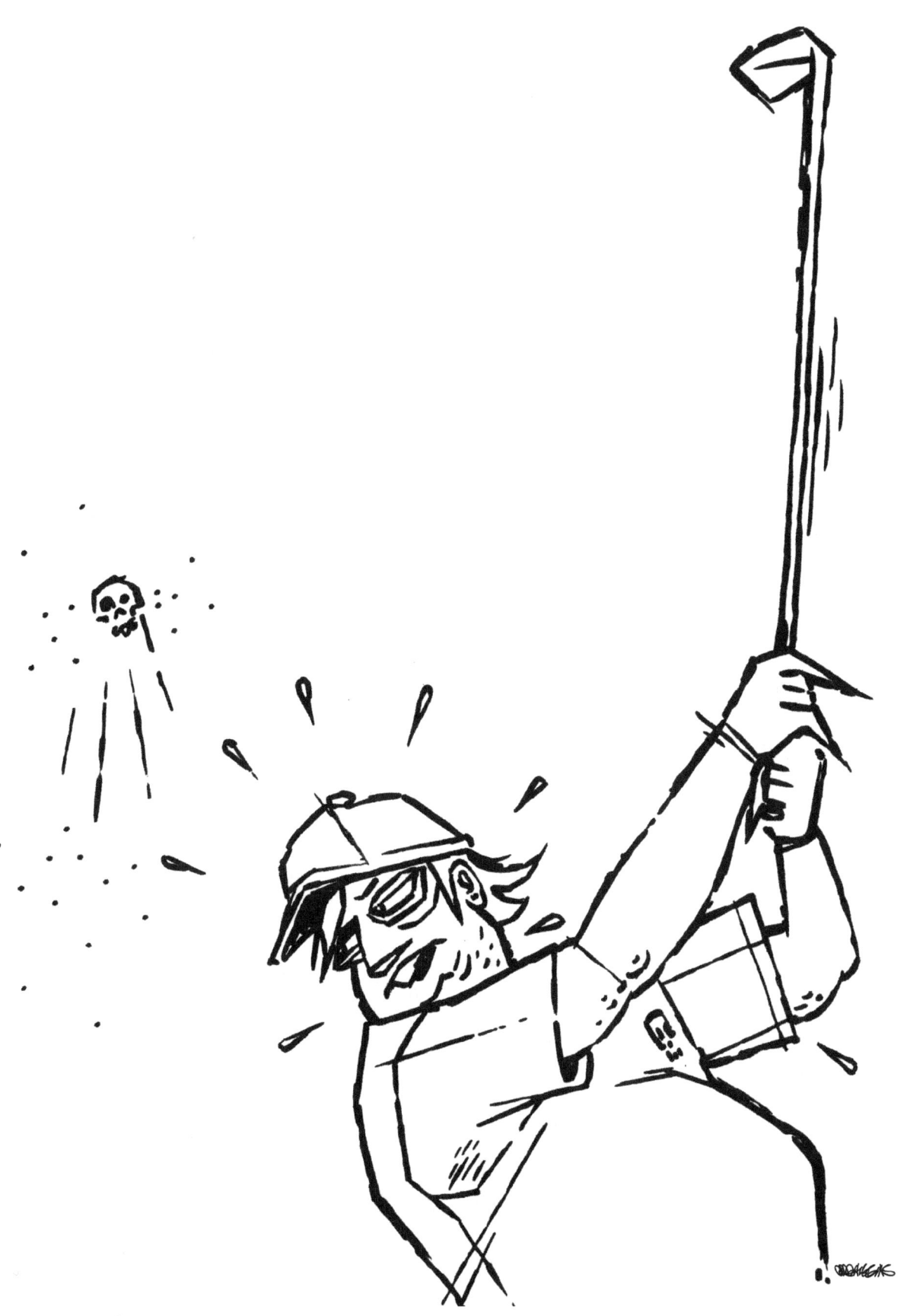

"I'm going to be working for you.
I'm not going to have time to go play golf."

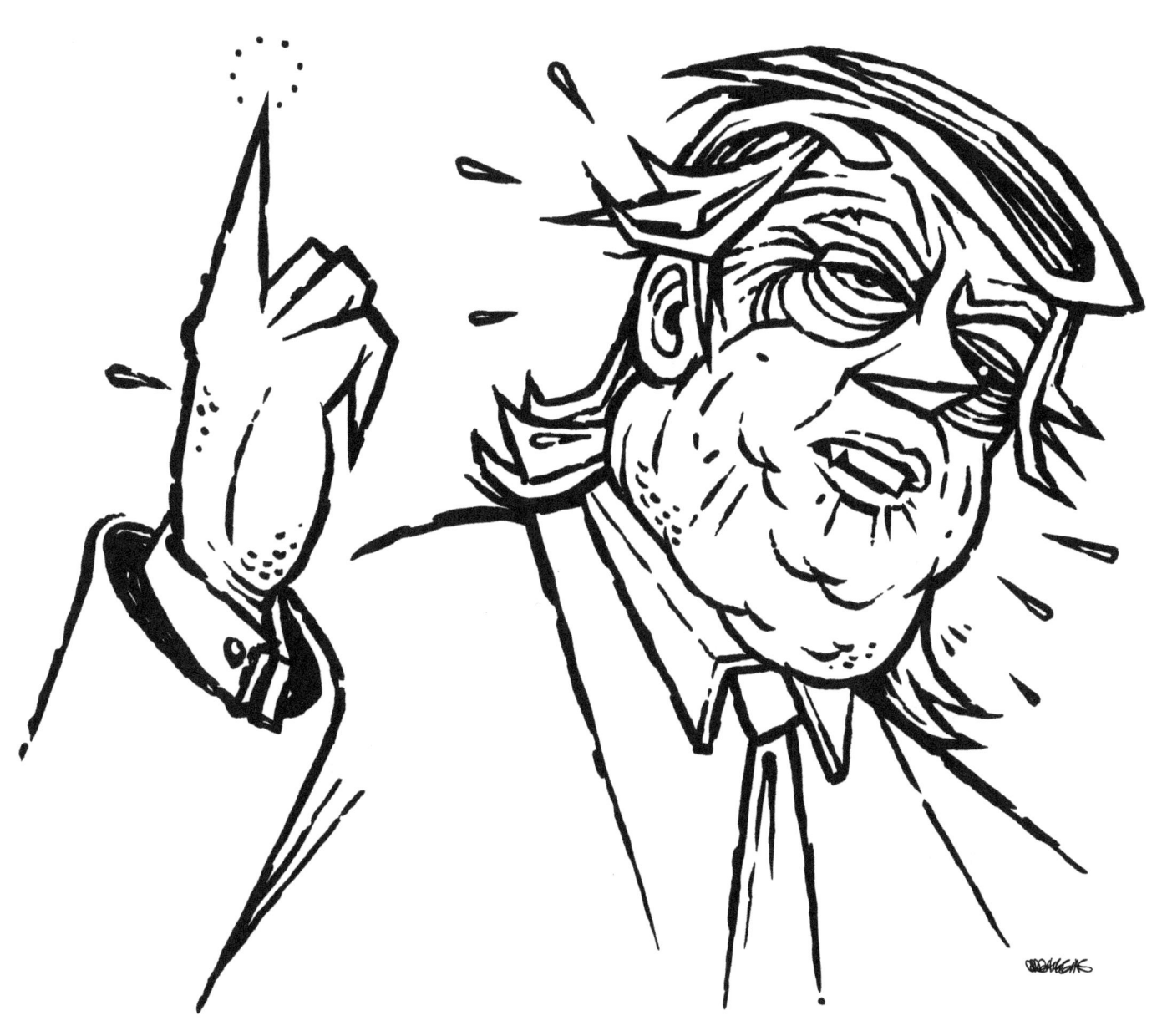

Color this asshole who embarasses his country with senseless rants over social media.

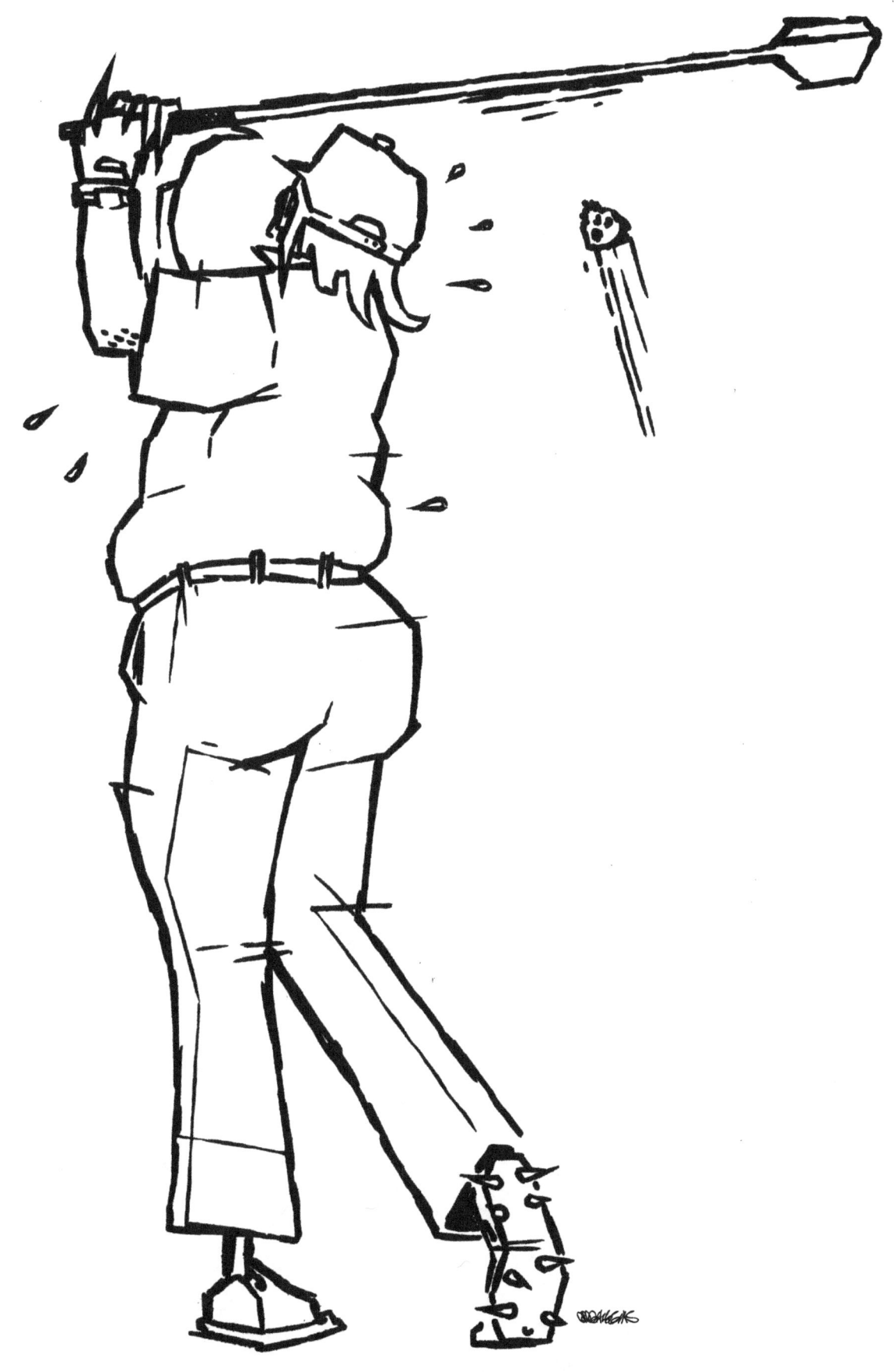
"I love the poorly educated."

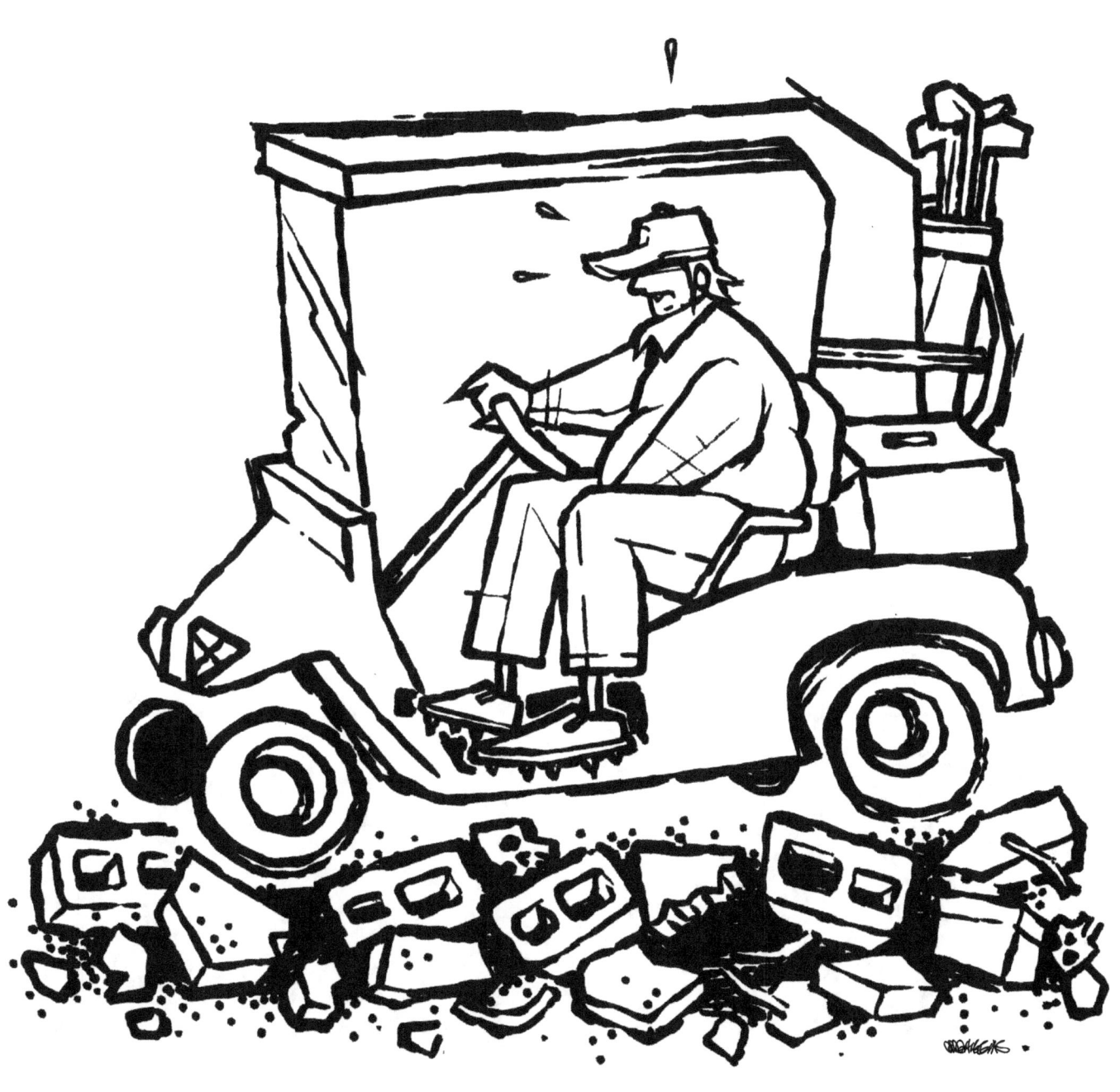

Color this asshole who said, "Why are we having all these people from shithole countries come here?"

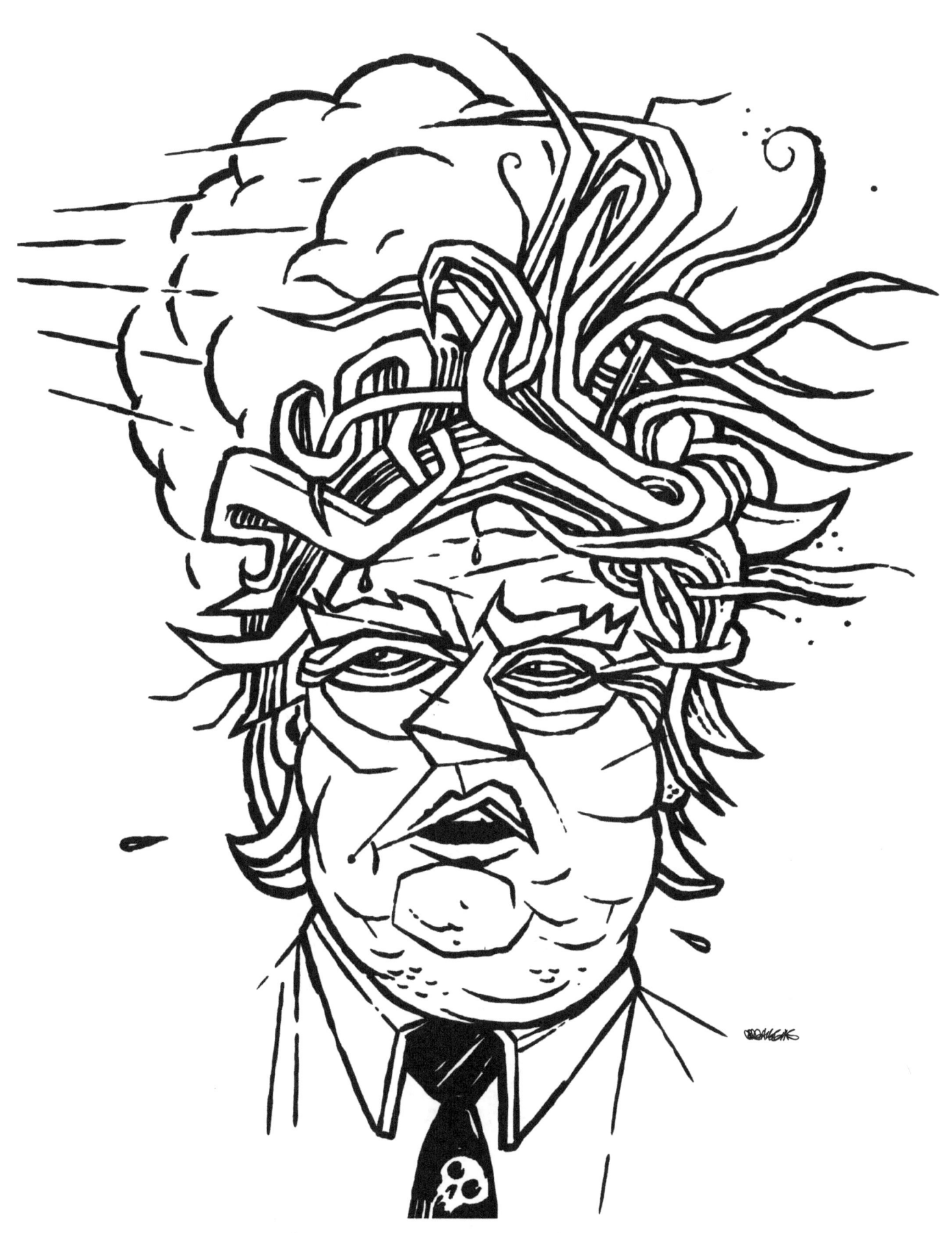

Color this asshole and his asshole hair.

www.ingramcontent.com/pod-product-compliance
Lightning Source LLC
Chambersburg PA
CBHW062234220526
45471CB00009B/3479